Zombie McCrombie
from an overturned Kombi

by Michael Ward

Illustrated by Gypsy Taylor

hardie grant books
MELBOURNE · LONDON

Dead yet alive
and hungry for brains
lurched Zombie McCrombie
from an overturned Kombi

and Montague Klutz
trailing his guts

with Zombie McCrombie
from an overturned Kombi.

Benedict Wise
enshrouded by flies,
Montague Klutz
trailing his guts

and Zombie McCrombie
from an overturned Kombi.

Lorelei Lisp
cooked to a crisp,
Benedict Wise
enshrouded by flies,
Montague Klutz
trailing his guts

and Zombie McCrombie
from an overturned Kombi.

Vladimir Snogg
walking the dog,
Lorelei Lisp
cooked to a crisp,
Benedict Wise
enshrouded by flies,
Montague Klutz
trailing his guts

and Zombie McCrombie
from an overturned Kombi.

Ichabod Grout
minus a snout,
Vladimir Snogg
walking the dog,
Lorelei Lisp
cooked to a crisp,
Benedict Wise
enshrouded by flies,
Montague Klutz
trailing his guts

and Zombie McCrombie
from an overturned Kombi.

Through rubble-strewn streets,
past an empty bus station
onward they shambled:
a mindless migration.
They sniffed at the wind
for bones they might gnaw,
when suddenly,
turning a corner
they
saw …

Five who'd survived,
locked
and
loaded.

'BOOM!'
went the guns.
'BOOM! BOOM!
BOOM! BOOM!'

In explosions of bone,
brain matter and gore
suddenly no-one
had heads anymore:
Ichabod Grout
minus a snout,
Vladimir Snogg
walking the dog,
Lorelei Lisp
cooked to a crisp,
Benedict Wise
enshrouded by flies,
Montague Klutz
trailing his guts

and Zombie McCrombie
from an overturned Kombi.

May they rest in pieces.

Published in 2015 by Hardie Grant Books

Hardie Grant Books (Australia)
Ground Floor, Building 1
658 Church Street
Richmond, Victoria 3121
www.hardiegrant.com.au

Hardie Grant Books (UK)
5th & 6th Floors
52–54 Southwark Street
London SE1 1UN
www.hardiegrant.co.uk

All rights reserved. No part of this publication may be reproduced, stored in a retrieval system or transmitted in any form by any means, electronic, mechanical, photocopying, recording or otherwise, without the prior written permission of the publishers and copyright holders.

The moral rights of the author and illustrator have been asserted.

Copyright text © Michael Ward
Copyright illustrations © Gypsy Taylor

A Cataloguing-in-Publication entry is available from the catalogue of the National Library of Australia at www.nla.gov.au

Zombie McCrombie from an overturned Kombi
ISBN 978 1 74379 017 5

Publishing Director: Fran Berry
Project Editor: Rachel Day
Design Manager: Mark Campbell
Production Manager: Todd Rechner